Robots at Home

BY NADIA HIGGINS

AMICUS HIGH INTEREST • AMICUS INK

Amicus High Interest and Amicus Ink are imprints of Amicus
P.O. Box 1329, Mankato, MN 56002
www.amicuspublishing.us

Library of Congress Cataloging-in-Publication Data
Names: Higgins, Nadia, author.
Title: Robots at home / by Nadia Higgins.
Description: Mankato, Minnesota : Amicus High Interest/
  Amicus Ink, [2018] | Series: Robotics in our world |
  Audience: Grades 4 to 6. | Includes bibliographical
  references and index.
Identifiers: LCCN 2016041971 (print) | LCCN 2016048580
  (ebook) | ISBN 9781681511450 (library binding) | ISBN
  9781681521763 (pbk.) | ISBN 9781681512358 (ebook)
  | ISBN 9781681512358 (pdf)
Subjects: LCSH: Robots–Juvenile literature. | Robotics–Juvenile
  literature.
Classification: LCC TJ211.2 .H46 2018 (print) | LCC TJ211.2
  (ebook) | DDC 629.8/93–dc23
LC record available at https://lccn.loc.gov/2016041971

Editor: Wendy Dieker
Series Designer: Kathleen Petelinsek
Book Designer: Tracy Myers
Photo Researcher: Holly Young

Photo Credits: Blue Frog Electronics cover; AutoPets 5; Gene
Blevins/Polaris/Newscom 6-7; SSPL/Getty Images 9; SRI/
Stanford Research Institute 10; Handout/KRT/Newscom 13;
Gunold/Dreamstime.com 14; Kyodo/AP Images 17; Eric
Piermont/AFP/Getty Images 18-19; AP Photo/Richard Drew
21; WikiCommons 22; Yonhap/EPA/Newscom 25; Georg
Wendt/picture-alliance/dpa/AP Images 26; EPA/European
Pressphoto Agency b.v./Alamy Stock Photo 28-29

Printed in the United States of America

HC 10 9 8 7 6 5 4 3 2 1
PB 10 9 8 7 6 5 4 3 2 1

Table of Contents

Dirty Jobs

What an odd robot. It just sits there in a corner, waiting. Then a cat steps inside. The robot wakes up. Its weight **sensors** tell it to get ready.

The cat does its business. Then it steps out. Soon, the ball slowly spins. Inside, kitty litter passes through a screen. The stinky clumps fall into a drawer. No one had to scoop! The robot does this dirty job.

Scooping cat litter is a job no one likes. But a robot doesn't mind doing it!

Machines at home are nothing new. How are robots different? They do their jobs on their own. They react to things around them. Many can do several kinds of jobs.

Robots are taking over all kinds of chores. They vacuum and mow. They wash windows. They can look out for burglars, too. They do jobs we do not like to do.

The Grillbot is a handy machine that can clean a barbeque grill.

Early Robots

To build robots, people needed three things: computers, electricity, and plastic. By the 1940s people had these things. A robot turtle named ELSIE could sense light. It could tell if it bumped into something. This simple robot found its own way around a room. This robot didn't do any jobs, but it let people see how robots could be built.

ELSIE was one of the first robotic machines. It helped lead the way for other robots.

Scientists used Shakey the robot to learn how to make robots better.

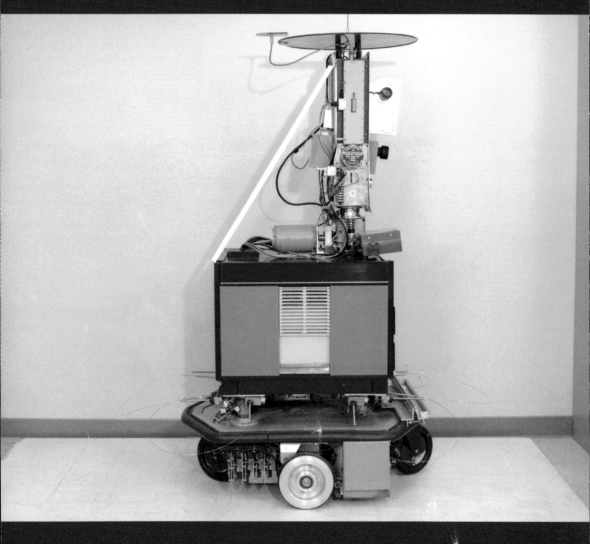

 How did Shakey get its name?

Shakey arrived in the 1960s. It was another robot built to do experiments. You could type in a command for Shakey. "Push the block off the platform." Shakey figured out the right steps to do it. **Engineers** tried to trick Shakey by closing doors or putting a box in the way. But Shakey found a new route. It did the job.

 People saw how it moved. It shook a lot when it started and stopped. Even still, people were amazed at what it could do.

Robot Helpers

Finally, in 2002, Roomba entered people's homes. This robot vacuums all by itself. Sure, a human **programs** in some rules. For example, "Don't fall down the stairs." But Roomba figures out how to move around stairs on its own. It can even move around a toy left on the floor.

 Does Roomba remember where it went?

Roomba can find its way around a room by itself. It sucks up dirt as it moves across the floor.

 Yes, newer models do. They make maps of the rooms as they go.

Don't worry. A Robomow can't work totally on its own. A person has to turn it on and tell it to go.

 **Q** How does a robot mower know to stay in the yard?

Robomow works like Roomba. But it mows grass instead of cleaning floors. Robots follow a cycle called sense, think, act. First, Robomow senses **data** about the world. For example, it might sense that something is in its way. The data goes to the computer. The computer thinks up a plan to turn around. Finally, the robot's wheels act out the plan. Robomow scoots the other way.

 A wire is buried around the edge of the yard. The robot can sense it like a fence.

It's one thing if a robot can sense a steep staircase. But what about seeing how a person feels? Pepper is a robot that can do that. Its cameras work together to see your face. It can tell if you look happy or sad. Pepper might someday be a robot friend in your home.

Pepper can roll around your home on its own. It can sense, think, and act.

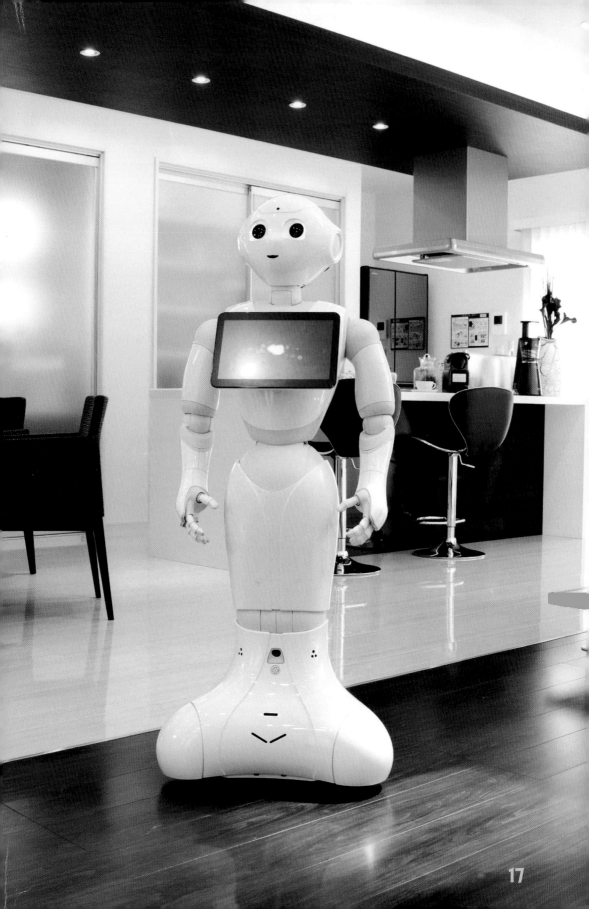

Buddy the robot is another helpful family friend. It finds you when it is time to get up. "Wake up," it says. "Don't forget it's Mom's birthday today."

Buddy can turn off lights or turn on the air conditioner. It can find your favorite song and play it. Buddy can even help practice math homework!

Buddy is a small robot. It's like a rolling tablet.

What Comes Next?

Today, more **home appliances** have computers. They have sensors. Many machines in homes can send messages to smart phones. One refrigerator has cameras. You can see what's inside on your phone while you are at the store. Maybe one day, your refrigerator could order groceries for you all on its own.

A touch screen on the front of a smart refrigerator lets people set reminders about food inside.

An early version of Asimo shows that robots can walk on stairs. It is one of few that can do this.

 Q What is a hard job for a robot?

How can robots be even more helpful? There are two main ways. For one, robots need to move better. Right now, robots work across flat spaces. Engineers are working on robots that can climb stairs and move over rough surfaces.

Second, robots are getting smarter. They follow voice commands. They recognize faces. They remember places. They can do complicated jobs.

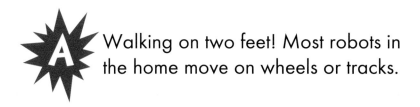 Walking on two feet! Most robots in the home move on wheels or tracks.

Mahru-Z is a robot maid. This **android** moves like a human. It has elbows and knees. It can wiggle its six fingers and two thumbs. Mahru-Z can look at something and know what it is. It picks up dirty socks. It puts them in the laundry. This metal maid can load a washing machine. It knows what buttons to push.

 Is Mahru-Z working in homes today?

Mahru-Z was built to practice making robots that can do many chores around the house.

 No. It is another experimental robot. Engineers hope it will show how robots could be a helper in space someday!

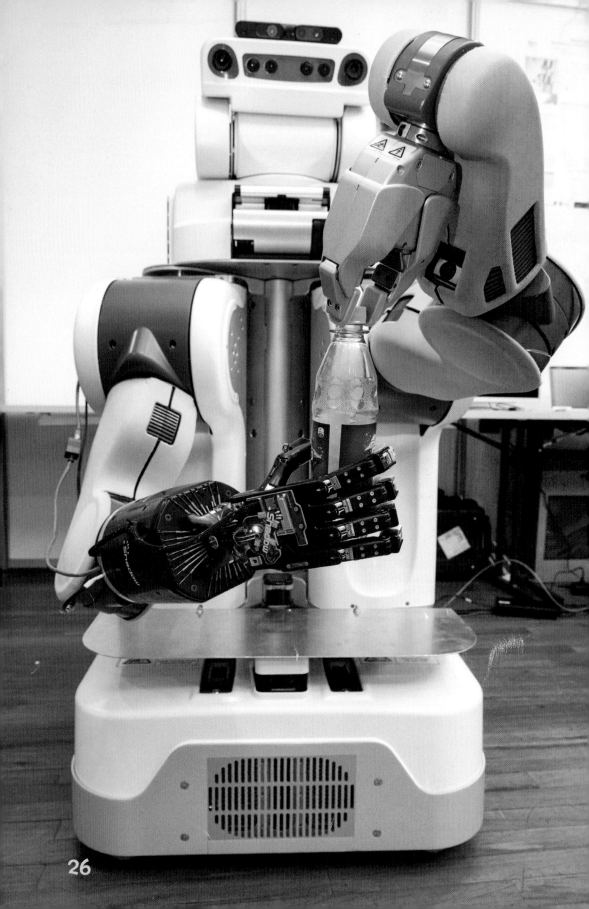

In 2015, PR2 amazed engineers. This robot made a cup of coffee. But PR2 had never seen the coffee machine before. It followed directions in plain English. PR2 had used other coffee machines before. It compared the new machine to what it already knew. It solved a problem the same way a human does. It shows that robots can learn.

PR2 can even open bottles. Scientists work to teach it lots of tasks.

A Robot in Every Home

Engineers keep building robots to practice with robotics. Asimo may be the smartest robot ever. It remembers you. You can talk to it like a human. It can even do sign language. The things it can do make it seem like a human. It makes it easy to imagine a robot that could do human jobs. Maybe someday, robot maids will be as common as coffee makers.

Asimo keeps learning new things. Today, it pours juice. What will it do tomorrow?

Glossary

android A robot in the shape of a human body.

data Information and facts about the world.

engineer Someone who designs and builds machines such as robots.

home appliances Machines in the home that help people do household chores, such as washing machines, blenders, dishwashers, and vacuum cleaners.

program To write a set of instructions for a computer or robot to follow.

sensor A robot part that can detect light, sound, or other things that we can detect with our five senses.

Read More

Furstinger, Nancy. *Helper Robots.* Minneapolis: Lerner Publications Company, 2015.

Leider, Rick Allen. *Robots: Explore the World of Robots and How They Work for Us.* New York: Sky Pony Press, 2015.

Swanson, Jennifer. *Everything Robotics: All the Photos, Facts, and Fun to Make You Race for Robots.* Washington, D.C.: National Geographic, 2016.

Websites

The DARPA Robotics Challenge
http://www.darpa.mil/program/darpa-robotics-challenge

Marco Tempest: Maybe the Best Robot Demo Ever
https://www.ted.com/talks/marco_tempest_maybe_the_best_robot_demo_ever

Index

About the Author

Nadia Higgins is the author of more than 100 books for children and young adults. She has written about everything from ants to zombies, with many science and technology topics in between. Higgins lives in Minneapolis, Minnesota, with her human family, pet lizard, and robotic dog.